God's Support

I can do everything God asks me to
With the help of Christ
Who gives me the strength and power.

Philippians 4:13

Reading the Bible Through Poetic Expression
How to Live a Life of Faith

Copyright © 2023 by Layne Case

ISBN: 979-8-9885146-1-9

To contact Layne Case, visit
www.amitypublications.com

ALEKA
ARTEMIS

Printed in the United States of America

READING THE BIBLE

THROUGH

POETIC EXPRESSION

How to Live a Life of Faith

Love
Hope
Faith
Gifts
Death
Worry
Family
Choices
Freedom
Marriage
Problems
Friendships
Thankfulness
God's Support
Encouragement
Following Christ
Being an Example
Peace

By Layne Case

Thankfulness

It is good to say
THANK YOU
To the Lord
To Sing Praises
To the God
Who is above all gods.

Psalm 92:1

CONTENTS

Hope

Everyone who asks...receives;
All who seek...find;
And the door is opened
To everyone who knocks!

Luke 11:10

FROM THE AUTHOR

For many years, I had been writing poetry to family and friends during times of challenges or celebrations. It was my "Hallmark" card with a personal message. I had always wanted to publish my poetry. When I began preparing the material for the book, I realized that each poem I had written had some reference to God, faith, or spirit. What was most interesting is while I had been writing these over a 25 year span, there were many periods of time when I was not attending a church or actively involved in my faith. But, clearly God still continued to inspire me to write. So, I decided to add scripture that would complement the reason I had written the poem. It was an amazing spiritual and faith building experience, one that taught me about what was in the Bible. In 2007, the book "Inspirations from My Family & Friends" was released. I continued to write poetry and in 2009, I published a second edition.

One year later, I wrote "Reading the Bible Through Poetry" Bible study. I researched scriptures that complemented different topics in life. The purpose was to help people learn where they could find scripture in the Bible that applied to every day issues. It also was a way to inspire others to worship but in a different format, to delve into a creative form of worship by writing poetry to express one's faith.

The study was the catalyst to the book "Reading the Bible Through Poetry – Second Edition" which includes the writings of students who participated in the study. The interpretations by individuals from different religious backgrounds were incredibly inspiring. Some of the participants were sure they would not be able to write poetry but each and every one found the words to express scripture in extremely meaningful ways.

So, I decided to publish this Bible study "Reading the Bible Through Poetic Expression" to help others who find the Bible overwhelming learn how to get through this life journey. Maybe you've heard "love your neighbor as you love yourself" and "ask and you shall receive." But how can you do this when life is throwing you one curve after another? Where can you find faith, hope, encouragement and peace during those times when you are scared, worried, and lost? When feeling thankful, grateful, joy and love, how can you share your blessings?

This study provides short scriptures that address many different topics. Participants are asked to read the scriptures listed for a particular week/topic, then choose one scripture that most inspires them. Participants will write their interpretation of the scripture in poetic format...stringing words together to form images, ideas and sounds that interpret scripture. This invites for a more creative writing experience. For those who think they do not have the skills to write poetry, the study includes a list of different types of poems from which to choose. Each writer's interpretation helps others to understand the Bible. The perspective through different eyes as well as the fact that each participant would be using a Bible of choice, gives greater insight into what the Bible teaches us about His plan for us.

My hope is that you will find support and guidance in the Bible as you deal with everyday life issues. The study is an opportunity to build your faith and self-awareness...helping individuals deal with issues that are weaknesses for themselves. It is not my intent to tell you how to live your life but to guide you through what God tells us about living a life of faith. It is for those who have never walked with God, for those just starting out on their journey, for those who are well along their way, or for those who desire to grow deeper in their faith. It is not just for poets and writers, but for anyone who seeks to know God and trusts Him, as an act of faith, by creating words in poetic format that will speak of your faith.

May you find peace as you walk this faith journey, giving God all the glory.

Layne Case

Choices

The Lord is good.
When trouble comes,
He is the place to go!

Nahum 1:7

WHAT YOU NEED TO KNOW

Resources Needed

- A Bible
- Notebook and pen/pencil
- "Reading the Bible Through Poetry–Second Edition (optional)

Study Length

The syllabus is broken into three sessions, six topics per session, with seven scriptures noted under each topic. Designed to be a weekly study, the length can be taught as an eight week study (intro, six topics, final), a fourteen week study (intro, twelve topics, final), or a twenty week study (intro, eighteen topics, final).

Participants

This study may be used as a daily devotional or group study. Any of the participants may serve as the leader or all participants may take turns leading each week. It is meant to help participants make time with God. It is not meant to replace or substitute any other study or worship time, but to augment what is already being done or it may be the study of your choice.

The study was designed to take 10-15 minutes of each day to stop and read the Bible, one scripture per day. However, participants may find that reading all the scriptures assigned each week at one time more beneficial.

It is highly recommended that each scripture verse be handwritten out. Handwriting activates a specific part of the brain which researchers believe is important to learning and memory. (www.verywellmind.com)

It is also recommended that the participant read the entire chapter, not just the verse listed. This helps to put the verse in context. Once all scriptures are read, choose one that is most inspiring, then select a type of poetry you will create. Multiple poems may be written but for time purposes, it is recommended that one poem be shared each week. Additional poems may be shared at the end of each session.

FORMAT

INTRODUCTION WEEK

Opening Prayer
Introductions
Each participant shares why they chose to attend.
Leader reviews purpose and study format.
Topic is identified for following week.
Questions
Prayer Concerns
Closing Prayer

TOPIC WEEKS

Opening Prayer
By Leader or Participants

Participants
Shares poem*

- Count to 10 before you recite your poem.
  - Please say nothing before you begin.
- Read your poem.
- Slowly and silently count to 5.
- Share the scripture chosen for that poem.
- Read your poem.
- Slowly and silently count to 5.
- Share the type of poem.
- Read you poem.

*This format is designed to help the listener "hear" the message. During the first reading, the meaning may be difficult to understand because one is "listening" vs "hearing." Once the scripture is identified, the second reading allows the listener to "hear" the interpretation. Most important is the interpretation of the scripture, followed by type of poem chosen.

Discuss how poem interpretations complement scripture.
Share any additional poems written.

Prayer Concerns

Closing Prayer
By Leader or Participants

FINAL WEEK

REFLECTIONS

Opening Prayer
By all Participants

"Following God gives me...."

Participants
Share poems
(Use the same format from topic weeks)

Topic/Scripture/Poem
Scripture/Topic/Poem

Prayer Concerns

Closing Prayer
By all Participants

"I am thankful for..."

The final week's assignment is an exercise in searching for scripture,
thinking of topics that are important to the participant, not what is
assigned, and creating a poem. It allows the writer to choose something
personal relative to their life. It is a powerful way to bring the study to
an end, gives the participants the knowledge to find ways to deal with
life's issues, and the opportunity to continue to build their faith in God.

Love

There are three things that remain…

Faith
Hope
Love

And the greatest of these is…

LOVE.

1 Corinthians 13:13

SESSION I

Week 1

TOPIC

Choices

SCRIPTURES

Proverbs 8:1-21
Joshua 24:15-28
1 Samuel 15:1-35
Proverbs 15:31-32
Matthew 13:47-52
Ecclesiastes 11:9-10
Deuteronomy 30:15-20

Choose one scripture and write, in poetic form,
what it means to you.

Week 2

TOPIC

Freedom

SCRIPTURES

Psalm 2:3-5
Genesis 3:1-24
Psalm 31:1-8
John 8:30-36
Romans 14:10-16
Galatians 5:1-6
2 Peter 2:19

Choose one scripture and write, in poetic form,
what it means to you.

Week 3

TOPIC

Friendships

SCRIPTURES

Proverbs 22:24-25
Genesis 14:14-16
Exodus 32:11-13
1 Samuel 20:30-34
2 Samuel 19:31-32
Proverbs 17:17
John 15:13-15

Choose one scripture and write, in poetic form,
what it means to you.

Week 4

TOPIC

Marriage

SCRIPTURES

Luke 16:18
Genesis 2:18-14
Genesis 24:67
Deuteronomy 24:5
Proverbs 6:32-35
Matthew 19:3-6
1 Corinthians 7

Choose one scripture and write, in poetic form,
what it means to you.

Week 5

TOPIC

Death

SCRIPTURES

Psalm 23
Ecclesiastes 9:10
2 Corinthians 5:8
Ephesians 2:8-9
Philippians 1:21-24
1 Thessalonians 4:13-14
1 John 4:17

Choose one scripture and write, in poetic form,
what it means to you.

Week 6

TOPIC

Faith

SCRIPTURES

1 John 5:4
Genesis 15:6
Matthew 8:5-13
Luke 17:6
Romans 4:3-5
Hebrews 11
1 Peter 3:13-15

Choose one scripture and write, in poetic form,
what it means to you.

Following Christ

Shine out among them
Like Beacon Lights

Philippians 2:15

SESSION II

Week 1

TOPIC

Example
Leadership

SCRIPTURES

Matthew 5: 14, 16*
Matthew 12:19-21
Mathew 20:26-28
Hebrews 12:1*
Titus 2:7*
James 3:13*
2 Timothy 1:7

Choose one scripture and write, in poetic form,
what it means to you.

Week 2

TOPIC

Encouragement
Future

SCRIPTURES

1 Thessalonians 5:11*
1 Corinthians 2:9
2 Corinthians 1:4*
2 Corinthians 13:11*
2 Peter 1:5-7*
Exodus 3:18-22
Genesis 12:1-4

Choose one scripture and write, in poetic form,
what it means to you.

Week 3

TOPIC

Family

SCRIPTURES

1 Kings 5:13-14
Psalm 127:1
John 19:25-27
Proverbs 11:29
Matthew 12:46-50
1 Timothy 5:3-5
2 Timothy 1:5-8

Choose one scripture and write, in poetic form,
what it means to you.

Week 4

TOPIC

Following Christ
God's Will

SCRIPTURES

Matthew 10:38-39*
Matthew 6:24*
Luke 9:23*
John 13:15*
Mark 8:34*
Philippians 2:13-16
Acts 16:6-10

Choose one scripture and write, in poetic form,
what it means to you.

Week 5

<u>TOPIC</u>

God's Support
God's Guidance

<u>SCRIPTURES</u>

Exodus 15:2*
Exodus 4:1-17
Ephesians 6:10-11*
Isaiah 41:13*
Philippians 4:19*
Psalm 16:1-8
Proverbs 13:13

Choose one scripture and write, in poetic form,
what it means to you.

Week 6

TOPIC

Love

SCRIPTURES

1 Corinthians 6:15
1 Corinthians 13:4-8, 13
Matthew 5:38-42
Matthew 23:37-39
Romans 8:35-36
Romans 12:9-21
Philippians 1:3-8

Choose one scripture and write, in poetic form,
what it means to you.

Peace

Always keep on praying.

1 Thessalonians 5:17

SESSION III

Week 1

TOPIC

Hope

SCRIPTURES

Genesis 8:1
Psalm 3:2-6
Mark 4:30-34
Joshua 10:25
1 Peter 1:3-6
Luke 18:35-43
1 Corinthians 15:53-58

Choose one scripture and write, in poetic form,
what it means to you.

Week 2

TOPIC

Worry

SCRIPTURES

Matthew 6:31-34
Matthew 8:23-27
Matthew 10:19-21
Luke 12:22-34
1 Corinthians 10:13
Philippians 4:4-7
Psalm 34:15-21

Choose one scripture and write, in poetic form,
what it means to you.

Week 3

TOPIC

Problems
Difficult Days

SCRIPTURES

Psalm 3:1-3
Matthew 11:27-30
Romans 8:26-28
 Thessalonians 1:5-8
Philippians 3:7-11
Philippians 4:6-7
James 1:2-4

Choose one scripture and write, in poetic form,
what it means to you.

Week 4

TOPIC

Thankfulness

SCRIPTURES

Leviticus 7:29
1 Chronicles 16:8-11, 23-25, 31-36
Psalm 92:1-5
Psalm 138:1-5
Luke 17:11-19
Acts 3:7-8
1 Thessalonians 5:16-17

Choose one scripture and write, in poetic form,
what it means to you.

Week 5

TOPIC

Gifts

SCRIPTURES

2 Chronicles 31:4-6
Nehemiah 10:36, 39
John 3:27-28
1 Corinthians 12:4-11
2 Corinthians 1:21-22
Ephesians 1:11
1 Timothy 4:14-16

Choose one scripture and write, in poetic form,
what it means to you.

Week 6

TOPIC

Peace

SCRIPTURES

Psalm 3:4-5
Psalm 4:6-8
Psalm 120:1, 7
Romans 5:1-2
1 Corinthians 1:3
2 Corinthians 13:11-12
1 Peter 3:10-11

Choose one scripture and write, in poetic form,
what it means to you.

Freedom

When someone becomes a Christian....
A new life has begun.

2 Corinthians 5:17

REFLECTIONS

Think of topics relative to your life
Find scriptures that address those topics.

CHOOSE TOPIC

Think about an issue you may need help working through.

IDENTIFY SCRIPTURE

Select scripture that addresses that issue.

WRITE POEM

Select a type of poem . Using that format,
choose words that reflect the meaning of the scripture.

TOPIC _____

SCRIPTURE_____

TYPE OF POEM_____

POEM

CHOOSE SCRIPTURE

Find scripture that is meaningful to you.

IDENTIFY TOPIC

Determine the topic being addressed in that scripture.

WRITE POEM

SSelect a type of poem . Using that format,
choose words that reflect the meaning of the scripture.

SCRIPTURE_____

TOPIC_____

TYPE OF POEM_____

POEM

Gifts

*God has given each of us the ability
to do certain things well.*

Romans 12:6

TYPES OF POEMS

Choose from the the list on the following pages.
Challenge yourself by selecting different formats.
Be inspired to create your interpretation of scripture.

ACROSTIC

- First letter of each line makes its own word or phrase vertically
- Rhyme or rhythm not needed
- Length of lines short or long

BALLAD

- Song-like poem with at least four stanzas, four lines each
- Tells a story and has action

COUPLET (cup - let)

- Two lines that rhyme
- Multiply couplets can be written to make one poem

DIAMANTE (dee – a – mahn - TAY)

- Seven lines written in the shape of a diamond
- 1st and 7th line have one noun.
- 2nd and 6th line include two adjectives describing nouns closest to them.
- 3rd and 5th line have three "ing" words related to those nouns.
- 4th line has four nouns, two related to first one, two related to the last one.

FREE VERSE

- No rhyme or format but has a free style rhythm.

HAIKU (hi - koo)

- Five five syllables for the first and third lines.
- Seven syllables for the second line.

SIMPLE RHYME

- Four lines with at least two of which rhyme.
- A B C B format
- B and B rhyme, but A and C do not.

SONNET

- Fourteen lines
- Three stanzas with four lines, one stanza with two lines
- Four line stanzas are in the A B A B rhyming pattern.
- Two line stanza is a couplet.
- Five stressed and five unstressed syllables in each line.
- First syllable of each line is not stressed.
- Stress sound is every other syllable

CINQUAIN^ (sin – kane)

- Five lines, unrhymed poem, twenty-two syllables
    - L1 - 2 syllables
    - L2 - 4 syllables
    - L3 - 6 syllables
    - L4 - 8 syllables
    - L5 - 2 syllables

NONET^ (no-net)

- Nine lines (rhyming is optional)
    - L1 - 9 syllables
    - L2 - 8 syllables
    - L3 - 7 syllables
    - L4 - 6 syllables
    - L5 - 5 syllables
    - L6 - 4 syllables
    - L7 - 3 syllables
    - L8 - 2 syllables
    - L9 - 1 syllable

ETHEREE^ (eh – ther – ee)

- Consists of ten lines
  L1 – 1 syllable
  L2 – 2 syllables
  L3 – 3 syllables...
  L10 – 10 syllables

- Reverse Etheree
  L1 – 10 syllable
  L2 – 9 syllables
  L3 – 8 syllables...
  L10 – 1 syllable

- Double Etheree
  L1 – 1 syllable
  L2 – 2 syllables
  L3 – 3 syllables...
  L9 - 9 syllables
  L10 - 10 syllables
  L11 - 10 syllables
  L12 – 9 syllables
  L13 – 8 syllables...
  L20 – 1 syllable

RONDELET^

- One verse, seven lines, **AbAabbA** format
- The capital letters - the refrains or repeats have four syllables (tetra-syllabic)
- Other letters – twice as long (octasyllabic) tetrameter.

(Sample)
Such Happiness

Copyright © 2003 Linda Newman

Such happiness
Has crept up on me without sound,
Such happiness
Has touched my heart with soft caress;
All life's sharp corners have gone round,
Since I've met you, my friend, I've found
Such happiness.

LANTURNE^

- Five line verse (shaped like Japanese lantern)
  Syllables – 1, 2, 3, 4, 1 per line

TRIOLET^

- Consist of eight lines
- 1st, 4th and 7th lines repeat
- 2nd and 8th lines repeat
- Rhyme scheme is AbaAabAB
  (*Capital letters represent the repeated line.*)
  AB repeated exactly
  a rhymes with ***A*** (line 1)
  b rhymes with ***B*** (line 2)

(Sample)

My Heart Residing in Thy Chest
(Copyright © 2003 Dan Tharp)

A(1)   For, break it shall and so it must

B(2)   My heart residing in thy chest

a(3)   When placed in care of lover's trust

A(4)   For, break it shall and so it must

a(5)   Passion's ashes returned to dust

b(6)   This lonely heart is laid to rest

A(7)   For, break it shall and so it must

B(8)   My heart residing in thy chest

^ Resource: www.shadowpoetry.com/resources/wip/types.html

Encouragement

If God is on our side,
Who can even be against us?

Romans 8:31

SAMPLES OF POEMS

By
Layne Case

CHOICES

Matthew 13
(Haiku)

The heart of a man
Shallow, thistled, hard or good.
How best to sow seed?

FREEDOM

Galatians 5
(Diamanté)

FRUIT

Sweet, Smooth

Nourishing, Satisfying, Fulfilling

Seed, Plant, Agape, Freedom

Soothing, Comforting, Caring

Kind, Gentle

LOVE

FRIENDSHIPS

1 Samuel 20
(Free Verse)

Friendships include loyalty.
Truth be told, loyalty is unshaken...
When it is for God.
HE will give us the wisdom
To make right choices.

MARRIAGE

1 Corinthians 7
(Free Verse)

Commitment...
To Christ brings stability.
To Faith brings reassurance.
To Love brings joy.
To Marriage brings fulfillment.
God is the foundation to
the success in our lives.

DEATH

1 Thessolonians 4
(Simple Rhyme)

At the end of life
The unsaved will be
Empty of hope
With nothing to see.

Yet, peace will be felt
When the ending is near
As those who are saved
Live without fear.

FAITH

Romans 4
(Haiku)

Being saved is free.
By believing, I am saved.
Faith will save my soul.

EXAMPLE

James 3
(Lanturne)

Speak
In truth
In kindness
When it's needed.
Speak.

ENCOURAGEMENT

Exodus 3
(Acrostic)

Exodus reminds us...

Nile became filled with blood.

Cattle died of plague.

Fr**O**gs came up from the water.

B**U**rning bush did not burn up.

Rod turned into a serpent.

Ashes caused boils.

Great hail destroyed crops.

Wat**E**r flowed from rock.

Swar**M**s of flies covered the land.

D**E**ath came to first born.

Nation infested with lice.

Ten Commandments were written.

FOLLOWING CHRIST

ACTS 16
(Acrostic)

Prepare to live a life with God.
Right thinking will clear the path.
Even in trouble times
Avoid living in fear.
Choose to live a clean life.
Healthy thoughts must prevail.

God so love the world.
Only through Him are we saved.
Obey His will.
Do unto others as God does unto us.

Never blame or complain.
Every one of us is a child of God.
When we act in love...
Surely a beacon of light will shine.

FAMILY

PROVERBS 11
(Triolet)

Grow trees that bear delicious fruit
With honest words of love and grace.
Building families from the root.
Grow trees that bear delicious fruit.
Continue daily in pursuit.
Keep joy and kindness upon your face.
Grow trees that bear delicious fruit
With honest words of love and grace.

GOD SUPPORT

EXODUS 15
(Etheree)

Live
With God
Unafraid.
Praise him daily.
Pray for salvation.
He is my light and strength.
He is in the songs I sing.
I will exalt Him forever.
I will not be afraid with God near.
Glorified Father of us all...Shine through.

LOVE

ROMANS 12
(Free Verse)

Wear an attitude of...
    Kindness shown to us by Jesus Christ.
Lay down your power and...
    Become a humble servant.
Dedicate your life to sharing...
    The love of Christ with others.
Honor and glorify the God...
    Who is our rock.
Stay strong in your beliefs...
    And your convictions.
And love, intensely, giving richness to others...
    In the most excellent way.

HOPE

MARK 4
(Lanturne)

Hope
Tiny
Mustard seed
With God in Sight
Lives

WORRY

MATTHEW 8
(Etheree)

God
Has Said
Don't worry.
I will save you
From the deep water.
When life's storms shake your world
Hold tight and know I am here.
Men of little faith, trust in me
For my Kingdom is yours. I will share.
I will provide all you need. Don't worry.

WORRY

LUKE 12
(Ballad)
By Barbara Burgess

When I was young, I learned to swim
So hard to win a race.
Though on the blocks, doubts filled my head,
Whether I could keep the pace.

And in my teens – late nights of study
To "ace" those final tests.
The future was calling LOUD to me,
Would I fail or be a success?

Those were the worries of my youth.
I wanted to win the GOLD.
As years passed by, more intense were they,
So many as I grew old.

I bit my nails; I drank the booze,
Seeking to relieve my pain.
Yet when I looked upward to my LORD,
I knew this was all in vain.

I've learned to pray my worries to God
And trust He'll see me through.
Just as he cares for the smallest birds,
I'm reminded, He loves me too!

PROBLEMS/DIFFICULT DAYS

MATTHEW 11
(Couplet)

Such a heavy yoke I wear
With the Father, I can bear.

THANKFULNESS

1 CHRONICLES 16
(Simple Rhyme)

Sing praises! Give thanks to the Lord
His might and his strength we must seek.
In a world that seems ready to fold
Lord, my God, help us. We are weak.

Heaven sings, earth rejoices, thanking you
As the seas roar in humbling praise.
Trees are waving and bowing in glory
Seeing wonder in the sky as we gaze.

Blessed to be one of God's precious children.
Spreading kindness and love to all
Singing triumphant sounds in His glory
O Jehovah, to our knees we will fall.

May we cherish and honor His name.
And be thankful for all that He's done.
With the love and compassion He shares
Thank you Father, Holy Ghost and The Son.

GIFTS

EPHESIANS 1
(Rondolet)

A gift to God.
Witnessing to others for Him.
A gift to God.
Teaching His word to those in need.
Blessed by the love He has shown you.
Chosen to share all the Good news.
A gift to God.

GIFTS

2 CHRONICLES 1
(Triolet)

Be generous in all you give.
Show honor to the Lord our God
For we belong to the Holy Spirit
Be generous in all you give.
Stand proud as a child of Christ.
He will give us all that we need
Be generous in all you give.
Show honor to the Lord our God.

PEACE

PSALM 4
(Cinquain)

I'm safe.
I will lie down.
I am never alone.
I always have God by my side.
In Peace.

2 CORINTHIANS 13
(Nonet)

The love of God is always with us.
Growing in Christ, we feel Him near.
As we foster amity...
Harmony and friendship...
Hearts open wide.
Goodwill to all.
Within us,
There is...
Peace.

REFLECTIONS

JOHN 15
Loyalty
(Diamanté)

Vine
Strong, Solid.
Bending, Connecting, Winding.
Rope, Branch, Flower, Food.
Nourishing, Fulfilling, Sustaining.
Sweet, Tasty.
Fruit

ROMANS 8
Assurance
(Sonnet)
By Jeff Hunt

Convinced and Assured

The promise of God for all who believe
No claim to divide, not seen as ending.
We claim Jesus Christ, new life we receive,
A gift, a truth, our hope never bending.

Like sheep to the slaughter, accounted as such
We travel our way down dangerous roads,
By Christ lifted up, we trust, oh, so much,
And by grace shoulder magnificent loads.

Nothing parts us from the love that Christ shares:
Not affliction, persecution or sword,
No nakedness, peril, famine even dares
When we wholeheartedly trust in God's word.

Triumphant we are through God's only son,
Rest assured our victory has been won!

Family

Unless the Lord builds a house,
The builders' work is useless.

Psalm 127:1

RESOURCES

Scripture passages referenced in this guide were taken from...

Life Application Bible for Students: The Living Bible, Tyndale House Publishing, Inc., 1992

*Promises & Prayers for Women Family Christian Press, 2006

BOOKS WRITTEN BY LAYNE CASE

Inspirations from My Family & Friends

Reading the Bible Through Poetry
Second Edition

Open Your Heart and Be Still

All books are available on Amazon.

Visit

www.amitypublications.com

to view other books
written by Layne Case and
published by AMITY Publications.

www.ingramcontent.com/pod-product-compliance
Lightning Source LLC
LaVergne TN
LVHW011429080426
835512LV00005B/349